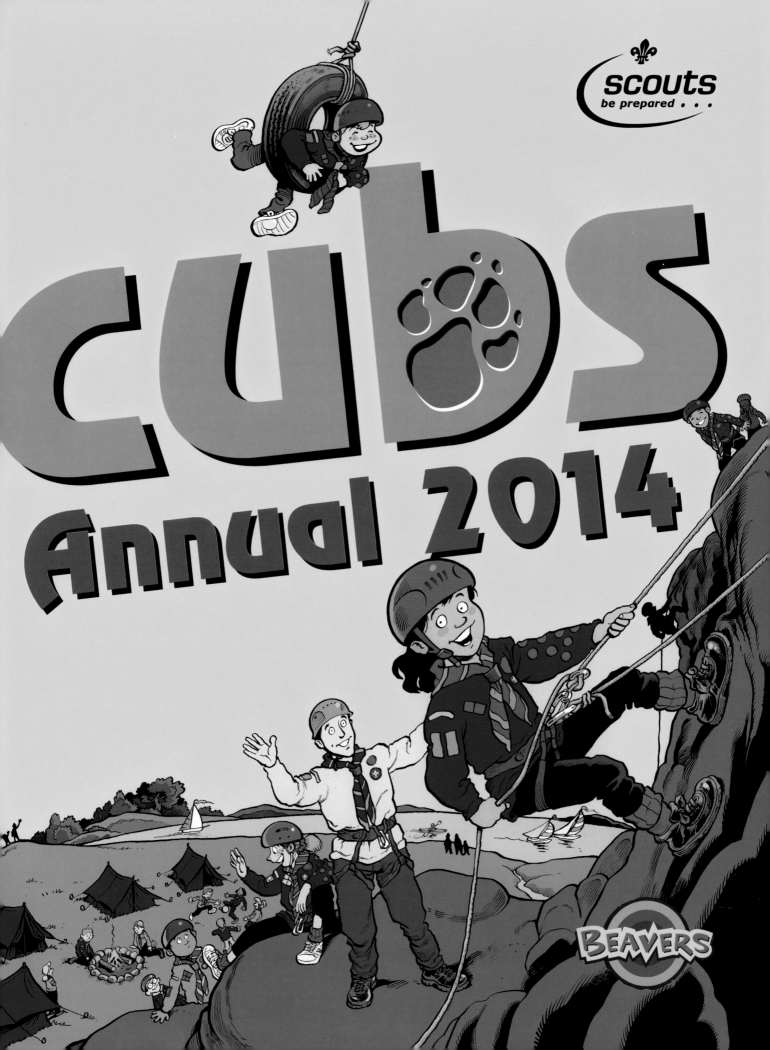

This annual belongs to:

Stick in a photo of yourself here – or draw a self-portrait!

. . . .

. . . .

I am . . . . years old.

I belong to the . . . .

. . . . Cub Scout Group.

I joined Scouting in 20 . . . .

Acknowledgements

Grateful thanks to Bear Grylls, Anita Meah-Wilson and the 14th Wimbledon Scout Troop (Cubs), Alex and Simon Edge, Rebecca Hooper and her family.

Author: Amanda Li

Designer: Dan Newman

Illustrator: David Parkins

Photography: Stuart Cox

First published 2013 by Macmillan Children's Books
a division of Macmillan Publishers Limited
20 New Wharf Road London N1 9RR
Basingstoke and Oxford
Associated companies throughout the world
www.panmacmillan.com

ISBN: 978-1-4472-2770-0

Hello there!

Do you get on with things or do you prefer to sit around waiting for them to happen? I always think that the world is divided into two types of people: those who think about doing things, and the people who actually do them.

The kind of people I'm talking about include Andrew Brown, who rowed across the Atlantic Ocean in 2011 or Dame Ellen MacArthur, who became the fastest person to sail round the world on her own. Or how about Jason Lewis, whose epic round-the-world journey took him 13 years to complete! Read about him on page 51. I once travelled around the whole of the UK on a jet ski – but luckily it only took me 30 days!

You don't need to go to such lengths, or at least, not yet. There's a world of adventure right on your doorstep. One of the best things about being a Cub Scout is getting an idea in your head and then making it happen. And the 2014 Cub Scout Annual has got plenty of ideas for you, from camping to pond safaris, food art to map making. There are also brilliant jokes and facts to amaze your friends. Did you know there are 300 other moons in our solar system as well as our own? Neither did I!

But the most important thing is to be a doer. It doesn't matter if things go wrong. You can always have another go. There's a great section at the start of this book called 'Seize the Day' – the world is out there, go and get it!

Your friend,

Bear

Bear Grylls
Chief Scout

'I LOVE ALL THE GAMES WE PLAY AT CUBS, ESPECIALLY DODGEBALL AND CRAB FOOTBALL.'

Jonty (8)

Contents

Seize the day!

Ever heard of the phrase 'Carpe Diem'? It's a famous Latin saying, which means 'seize the day'. In other words, make the most of every single day to do something fun, memorable and exciting. Here are some awesome ideas for things to do, both outdoors and indoors.

Learn something new

Set yourself a challenge to learn something that you've never done before. How about:

- **Juggling** – start with two balls or bean bags, then work your way up to three. Practice makes perfect!
- **Learn to say 'Hello'** in several different languages. How about Spanish – 'Hola!' – or Chinese – 'Nee Haow'. You'll be welcomed all over the world!
- **Master something tricky** – how about a cartwheel, a handstand, a new swimming stroke or skipping with a rope? (See page 19 for lots of helpful skipping tips.)
- **Make a list of skills you'd like to learn,** from skateboarding to singing to sign language. Then devote ten minutes every day to practising your skill. With hard work and determination you will eventually master it.

Get that badge!

Drawing a local map and visiting a place of interest could help you get your **Cub Scout Local Knowledge Activity Badge**.

Draw a map of your local area

Get some paper, a pencil and a rubber and think carefully about where you live. Start off by drawing your house and work from there, sketching out all the local roads and paths. Write the names of the streets along them. Now add on the local schools, shops, library, parks, bus stops, stations and any other features or places of interest.

Whenever you visit a new place in your local area, you can add it to your map.

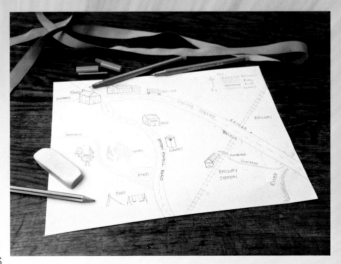

Be a spy for a day

Go undercover and become a secret agent for a day. First you will need a fake identity, so invent a super spy name. Then make yourself a pretend passport using your new name, a drawing or photo of yourself and your fingerprints. Next, on to some surveillance skills – see if you can quietly follow a family member or friend around the house or garden *without* being seen! Then it's time to crack some codes. Invent your own code and write a secret note. If you do this activity with a friend you can swap notes afterwards and try to decipher them.

Make up a funny show

Why don't you make up a hilarious show or sketch with your friends? Just think of something that makes you all giggle – and take it from there! Or get a joke book, memorize the best jokes and perform them to an audience. You might just end up as the star of your next Cub Scout show!

Get that badge!

Taking part in a show can help you get your **Cub Scout Entertainer Badge**.

Make a time capsule

Wouldn't it be great to discover a time capsule, full of interesting things from times gone by? What about making one for someone else to find – maybe even one of your future grandchildren! To do this, you will need a good-sized waterproof container with a tight fitting lid – a used biscuit tin is ideal. Now gather together any interesting items you can find – how about a page from the day's newspaper? A coin or some small change? A list of important facts about the world today? Also put in something personal about you – maybe a photograph or a tracing of your hand. You could include a list of your current favourite songs, movies and books and write a message to the 'future you'!

When it's finished, either bury your time capsule in the garden or hide it somewhere in the house. Put a label on the time capsule saying 'DO NOT OPEN BEFORE . . .' and write in a future date, a very long way off!

Create a treasure hunt

Why not make up a fun treasure hunt for your friends? Treasure hunts can be outdoors or indoors – it's up to you – and the weather, of course. But first you'll need some treasure! Choose a suitable 'prize' and hide it. Now you need to make up some clues. Write them on pieces of paper or card and hide them in different locations.

Each clue should lead to another, making a trail that will eventually get to the prize. For example, 'Find me in the smallest room in the house' could lead to the bathroom, where another clue will be hidden to the next location. If you're outdoors 'Find a place like a beach but without any sea' could be a sandpit in the park.

Build a den

One of the simplest ways to build a den is to find a tree with a branch sticking out at about 'ceiling' level. Then you'll need to look for lots of branches and twigs to lie against the branch to create a kind of tent. You can stuff any gaps with leaves and moss. All your hard work will be worth it when you stand back and admire your fantastic outdoor den!

If it's raining outside, you can have lots of fun building an indoor den, using a table, chairs, a clothes airer and maybe a broomstick or two. Drape old blankets, sheets or towels across and over the furniture and you've got yourself a secret hideaway.

Make a musical instrument

Take a look in your recycling crate and see what you can use to make a simple instrument. Here are some ideas:

- A drum from a plastic tub or yogurt pot, with paper or cling film stretched across the top.
- Maracas from lidded containers filled with dried beans or rice.
- A trumpet from the inside tube of a kitchen roll. Cover one end with paper and an elastic band, then make a row of holes along one side of the tube with the tip of a pen. Hum into the open end.
- A kazoo from a comb with a piece of tissue paper folded over it.
- A guitar from a shoe box lid and some large elastic bands stretched over it.

Why not make them all and start a band!

Take one tent . . .

Have you ever been camping? Part of the fun is spending the night inside your very own tent.

Experienced Scouts know that when you're spending the night outdoors, your tent is really important. It needs to be tough enough to shelter you from all kinds of weather and comfortable enough to let you have a good night's sleep. Putting up a tent (and putting it away) is something every Cub Scout should learn to do too.

Traditional tents come in lots of different shapes and sizes. Here are just a few tent types. Do you recognize any of them?

Ridge tent

A ridge tent has a horizontal pole going across the top of it with one or two upright poles to support it.

Dome tent

These are bubble-shaped tents which have hoops criss-crossing inside them. Because of their rounded shape, water rolls off them easily.

Tunnel tent

As its name suggests, this tent is shaped just like a tunnel and has two or more hoops supporting its length.

'CAMPING IS BRILLIANT. IT'S LIKE A BIG SLEEPOVER, BUT MUDDIER!'

Joe (9)

Bell tent

The bell tent is supported by a single pole in the middle of the tent.

Yurt

A yurt is a traditional tent made from felt or animal skins over a wooden framework. Yurts are used by nomads (travelling people) in Mongolia and Central Asia.

Tipi

A tipi (or teepee) is a pyramid-shaped tent made from wooden poles tied together and covered with animal skins. Tipis were originally used by Native Americans.

'TAKING DOWN THE TENT WAS QUITE HARD UNTIL OUR LEADER SHOWED US HOW TO DO IT!'

Theo (9)

Get that badge!

Learning how to pitch a tent can help you get your **Cub Scout Camper Activity Badge**

The tent of the future

Have you ever seen a tent like this? This incredible tent has got an impressive list of features, including:

- wind turbines to catch the wind and turn it into power
- solar panels to turn sunlight into electricity
- a portable battery for charging electronic devices
- an 'intelligent' sleeping bag that regulates your body temperature
- solar-powered baseball caps with built-in torches for bedtime reading!

Would you like to spend a night in this tent?

My top tent

If you could design your own unique tent, what would it look like? What sort of useful features would it have? And what would you put in it for fun? Draw and describe your ideal tent here.

Help! Camp crisis!

All camping trips need to be well-organized.
Take a look at this crazy – and dangerous – campsite!
Can you find ten things that might go wrong?

Answers on page 62.

Wrap it up!

You don't need lots of pots and pans to cook a delicious dinner outside.

All you need is some tasty food, a fire and foil or newspaper. Here are some great recipes for you to try on your next camping trip – let's wrap it up!

IMPORTANT: You must always have a grown-up helper with you when you're cooking outside. Knives and open fires can be dangerous – your helper will need to do any cutting or hot food handling.

Top tips for outdoor cooking

- Check that you've got everything you need before you start – food, foil, cutlery, bowls, tongs and a tea towel or oven gloves.
- Spray oil is really useful, as it is not as messy as oil from a bottle or butter.
- The best kind of fire for cooking is a fire that has turned to glowing embers. You will need to get the fire going at least half an hour before you start cooking. Keep the embers hot by adding small amounts of wood at regular intervals.
- Tongs are really useful for cooking food outdoors – you can pick up and turn over food without burning your hands!
- When cooking with foil, use two layers to prevent any leaks.

Fish in newspaper

You will need:
- One fresh fish fillet per person
- Pieces of greaseproof paper – one for each fillet
- Several old newspapers
- Scissors or knife (take care)
- Tongs
- Salt, pepper and herbs
- Large bowl of clean water
- String

How to do it:
1 Take the newspaper and lay out six sheets in a pile for the first fish fillet.
2 Season the fillet with salt, pepper and herbs and wrap it in greaseproof paper.
3 Place the wrapped fish in the centre of the newspaper and wrap the fillet up securely, tying it firmly with the string.
4 Place the parcel in the bowl of water until the paper is wet through.
5 Take the parcel out and gently squeeze out any excess water.
6 Place the damp parcel on the hot embers and turn every five minutes, using tongs. The fish should be cooked by the time the paper begins to get blackened: about 20–30 minutes. Splash extra water on the parcel if the edges of the paper start to smoke.
7 Cut open the parcel and dig in to the delicious cooked fish!

Campfire omelette

You will need:

- Eggs – two per person
- A small amount of butter or spray oil
- Grated cheese, chopped ham, chopped tomatoes or other fillings
- Plastic bowl and fork
- Foil

How to make

1 Tear off two pieces of foil (about 20–25 cm across) and shape them into a 'bowl'. Grease or spray the inside of the bowl with the butter or oil.

2 Break the eggs into the plastic bowl and beat well with the fork.

3 Pour the beaten egg into the foil bowl and add the fillings of your choice.

4 Place the foil bowl on the hot embers and watch your omelette cook!

5 Remove the bowl with care and let it cool down. Now you can eat your tasty omelette straight from the foil.

Bag it up

You can cook lots of things in foil. Just place your prepared fish, meat, fruit or vegetables on to a couple of foil sheets. Add salt, pepper, herbs and butter or oil, and wrap it up carefully, like a bag. Seal the edges of the foil really tightly by rolling them over. Place the foil bag on the embers and turn it over every few minutes as it cooks. Check to see that the food is properly cooked before eating! Seal it up again well if it needs more cooking time.

For delicious **roasted veggies**, use any combination of your favourite vegetables – try chopped potatoes, carrots, onions, mushrooms, courgettes and peppers. A grown-up can help you cut the vegetables or bring them pre-cut from home.

What's your favourite food to eat on a camping trip?

Did you know?

If you don't have any foil you can sometimes use cabbage leaves instead. If you lay large cabbage leaves over the hot embers you can spray them with oil and put fish, meat, fruit or vegetables on top of the leaves to gently cook. Always make sure your meat and fish is really well-cooked all the way through before you eat it.

Finally, to finish your meal, how about a mouthwatering . . .

Pear and chocolate dessert

You will need:
- One ripe pear for two people
- Chocolate – either in a bar or a bag of chocolate chips.
- Foil

How to do it
1 Ask your adult helper to carefully cut the washed pear in half. Scoop out the core from each half.

2 Place each pear half on a piece of foil big enough to wrap around it.
3 Place some of chocolate, or chocolate chips, into the hollow of each pear half.
4 Wrap the pears up and place in the embers for 20–25 minutes or until the pears are soft.
5 Unwrap and enjoy the smell of the melted chocolate – mmm! Let it cool a little, then tuck into your delicious warm dessert.

Get that badge!
Preparing and cooking an outdoor meal can help you get your **Cub Scout Camper Activity Badge**.

Try these tasty but tricky brainteasers!

Puzzling food

```
D S N K S T T D D
L C A N U O E A P
F F A U M B Q E O
I E Y A S F I R T
B R T O N A J B A
N O C A B O G X T
D B V E S M I E O
E G G G Z L D N Y
E G N L Z F U J O
```

Sizzling search

Find all the ingredients for a fabulous campfire fry-up. The words might be up, down, diagonal or backwards. Good luck!

Sausage   Bacon

Egg   Potato

Tomato   Onion

Bread   Beans

Fruit sudoku

Can you fill in the spaces with a banana, apple, strawberry or grapes? But there's an important Sudoku rule – each of the four fruits must appear only once in each row (across) or column (down).

Greedy grid

Find out what the campfire snack is by completing this word grid. All the words are things you can eat. Yum!

Fill in one letter on each line to make two words. The missing letter will be the last letter of the first word, and also the first letter of the second word, e.g. H A **M** U S H R O O M.

SOU ▢ EA

CHEES ▢ GG

PAST ▢ PPLE

FLOU ▢ ICE

Answers on page 62.

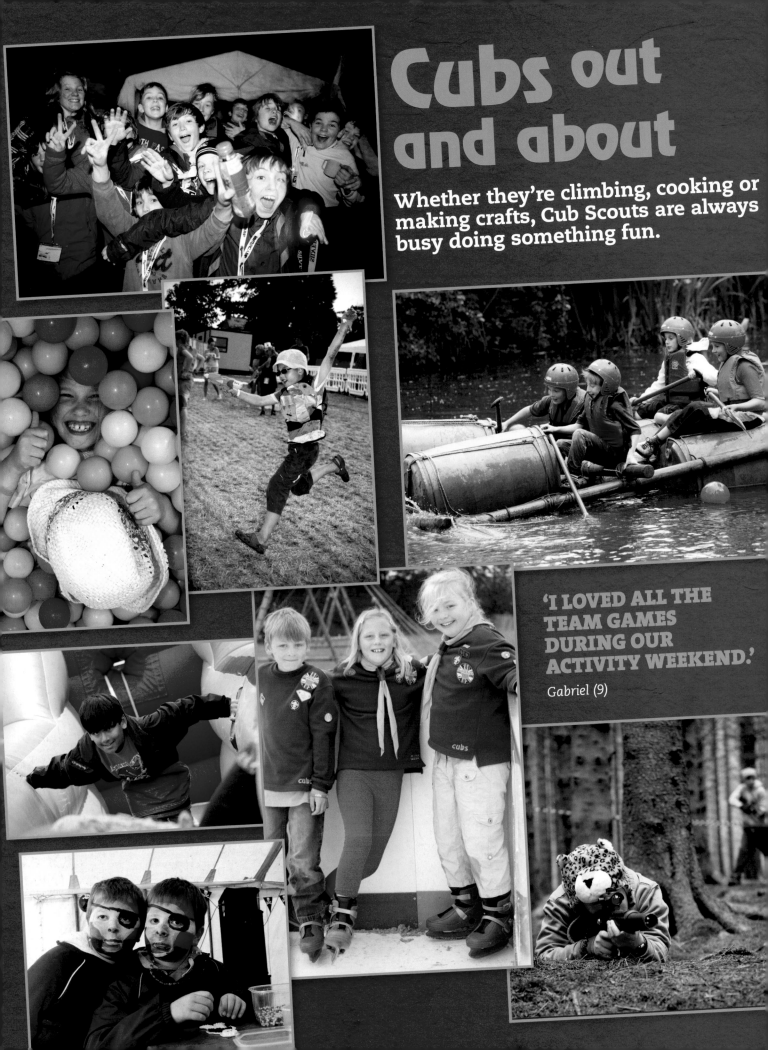

Cubs out and about

Whether they're climbing, cooking or making crafts, Cub Scouts are always busy doing something fun.

'I LOVED ALL THE TEAM GAMES DURING OUR ACTIVITY WEEKEND.'

Gabriel (9)

'THIS YEAR
I'VE DONE
ROCK CLIMBING,
ARCHERY
AND TARGET
SHOOTING.'

Joe (9)

Hop, skip and jump!

You'll need balance, strength and agility to master these games and activities.

Hop till you drop!

Some historians think that hopscotch dates back to Roman times, when soldiers may have played the game to practise their footwork and balancing skills. If you've ever tried it, you'll know that it's not as easy as it looks!

How to do it:

Use a hopscotch area in a playground or draw your own game with chalk, like this:

Find a small stone, coin or other small object to play with. Throw your stone on to the first number – 1. If it touches the line or lands outside the square, you miss a turn. If it's safe, start hopping and jumping!

Hop or jump on to every square *except* the square your stone is on – the 1. Hop onto the single squares – 4, 7 and 10 – and jump with two feet on to all the double squares. If you touch the line or your foot goes outside the square, you are out until your next go.

If you get to the end – hop on to 10 – do not put your foot down! (If you do, you're out till the next turn.)

You must turn around *hopping* while still on one leg, and go all the way back to the start.

When you reach 3 and 2, bend over and pick up your stone from number 1, then jump over it. Now you have to do it all over again, throwing your stone on number 2 – it's more difficult, as this time you'll have to hop *around* it, using 1, 3 and 4. And you have to pick the stone up from a hopping position on the way back!

Keep going until you do something wrong. Then it's the other player's turn. When it's your turn again, start from the number you stopped at last time.

The first person to reach number 10 – *and make it back* – is the winner!

Super skipping

Skipping with a rope can be tricky to learn at first. But once you've mastered it, it's a fantastic way of keeping fit. That's why many athletes and boxers are keen skippers.

Check your skipping rope is the right length by standing on it and pointing the handles upwards. They should not be higher than your shoulders or lower than your waist.

Now for the skipping. Hold your rope and swing your arms from behind you, bringing the rope over your head. Jump when you see the rope fall and you will hopefully jump over it. If you tread on the rope, just keep on practising – you'll soon get the hang of it! Big arm movements and high jumps aren't necessary. Try to turn the rope using mainly your forearms and wrists and jump low.

Once you've mastered the basic skip, try some fancy footwork:

The scissor jump

When you jump, land with one foot forward and the other foot some way behind it. When the rope comes down again, change your legs over, so that you make a scissor movement. Keep going as long as you can. Try to land on the balls of your feet and lean forward to keep your balance.

Around the world

Try to make a complete circle by jumping in one direction. Take one jump, then turn your body for the next jump. Keep going in a circle shape, jumping a bit further round each time until you are back to the original position.

Can you go 'around the world' in just five jumps?

Jump to it!

Jump the stream

You will need:

- Two long pieces of string (or two sticks)

How to do it:

Lay the strings parallel to each other, just 20 or so cm apart – an easy jump to start with.

Players line up. Their challenge is to jump over the 'stream' without getting wet. They mustn't touch the strings at all.

After everyone has had a go, move the strings further apart – making it more difficult to jump across. Players who touch the string are 'wet' – out of the game. Keep moving the strings further apart, until there is only one 'dry' person left!

Another way of playing this game is 'hop the stream' – just hop instead of jumping!

Team skipping challenge

For this you need an extra-long piece of rope. Two people are the rope turners and stand opposite each other. The other players line up and take turns to jump in and skip. You can make rules such as everyone has to do two, three or four skips before jumping out, or you can try and get more than one person skipping at a time! The important thing is for the rope turners to keep the rope turning at the same beat so that the skippers know what to expect.

Coffee and Tea

This traditional skipping rhyme for two looks simple but takes some skill!

'I like coffee, I like tea.
I like (friend's name) to jump with me.'

(The friend now jumps in so that two of you are jumping at the same time.)

'1, 2, 3, change places, 4, 5, 6, change places, 7, 8, 9, change places . . .'

(The two jumpers swap positions each time they say 'change places'.) Keep going for as long as possible and see what number you can reach before one of you steps on the rope!

The Sargent Jump challenge

The Sargent jump is a test of muscle strength and power. It is named after its inventor – Dr Dudley Sargent – who created it in 1921. It is also known as a vertical jump test.

The object is to jump as high as you possibly can from a standing position.

You will need:
- A wall
- A tape measure
- A piece of chalk
- A grown-up helper

How to do it:
Make sure you warm up well and do a few practice jumps before you start.

Put some chalk on to the end of your fingers.

Now stand sideways to the wall, keep both feet flat on the ground, and reach up with the hand that is closest to the wall. Make a chalk mark on the wall with your fingers. This is called your 'standing reach height'.

Now for the jump! Stand a little bit away from the wall and jump as high as you can, using the power of your arms and legs to help you. As you jump, touch the wall at the highest point that you can with your chalky fingers.

Now ask your grown-up helper to measure the distance between the two marks. Write your measurement in centimetres on the table to the right.

Can you do even better? You have three chances to jump as high as you can and to try and get the longest measurement. Which will be your best score?

Get that badge!
The Sargent Jump is one of the jumps you can perform to gain a **Cub Scout Athlete Activity Badge**. You can also do skipping, running and lots of other activities – so get moving!

MY JUMPS

Jump 1

Jump 2

Jump 3

21

Let's go on a pond safari

Ponds can be a real haven for wildlife. So let's get dipping!

Ponds are fascinating places, full of tiny creatures that are hard to spot. Take a closer look and you'll discover a world of wildlife you've never seen before.

Before you start
Pond dipping can be messy – and wet! So wear clothes that you don't mind getting muddy and roll up your sleeves.

You will need:
- A pond or stream
- A small net with a handle
- A container – a shallow tray works well but a washed ice cream container is just as good
- A magnifying glass – to look at minibeasts more closely
- Identification chart – see page 23.
- A notebook and pencil – to record your finds
- A grown-up helper

Pond safety
1. Always do pond dipping with a grown-up helper, **NEVER** on your own.
2. *Kneel down* at the edge of the water when you are dipping. This will help you keep your balance. If you lean over the water while standing up, you might fall in.
3. Pond water can carry diseases so never get water in your mouth or eyes. Always wash your hands well with soap and water after you have been pond dipping.
4. The minibeasts you will catch are delicate, so be gentle and don't pick them up with your hands. When you've finished looking at them, put them carefully back in the pond.

STAY SAFE NEAR WATER!

Perfect pond dipping
Fill up your tray or container half full with pond water and place nearby.

Put your net slowly into the water and gently sweep it around for a few seconds. The best places to find minibeasts are close to plants or at the edges of the pond.

Bring the net out of the pond and take it to your container.

Turn the net inside out very carefully so anything you've caught slips smoothly into the container water.

Look carefully at anything that is moving and check it against the pond chart. A magnifying glass is useful, as many of the creatures are very tiny.

My pond identification chart

What have you found? Tick the box if you have discovered any of these creatures.

Not drawn to scale

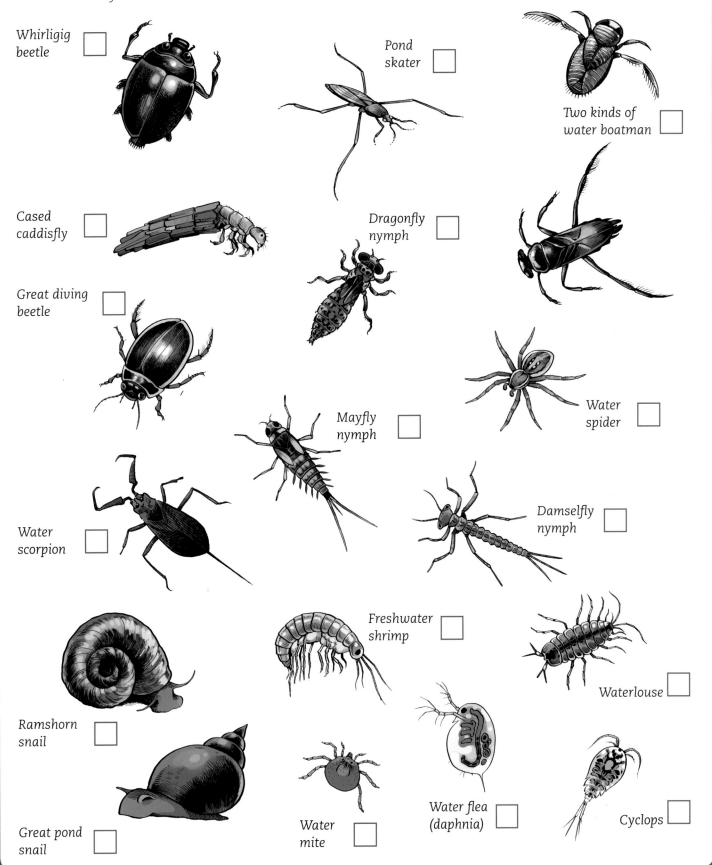

Whirligig beetle ☐

Pond skater ☐

Two kinds of water boatman ☐

Cased caddisfly ☐

Dragonfly nymph ☐

Great diving beetle ☐

Mayfly nymph ☐

Water spider ☐

Water scorpion ☐

Damselfly nymph ☐

Freshwater shrimp ☐

Waterlouse ☐

Ramshorn snail ☐

Water mite ☐

Water flea (daphnia) ☐

Cyclops ☐

Great pond snail ☐

23

What have you found?

Choose your favourite minibeast out of all the ones you have found. How many legs has it got? Does it have wings or a shell? Do you think it will turn into something else? Draw and describe your minibeast.

Frogs in the pond

When you've finished pond dipping, why not play this game with your friends?

Make a large circle on the floor – use rope, masking tape or draw it with chalk. This is the 'pond'.

The players – the 'frogs' – stand in a circle around the edge of the pond.

When the leader shouts 'In the pond!' all the frogs jump over the line and into the circle.

When the leader shouts 'On the bank!' the frogs jump outside the circle, back to where they started.

Listen carefully! If the leader says 'In the bank' or 'On the pond', nobody moves. Any frog who moves at the wrong time is OUT and must sit down! Last person left is the winner.

What's in the pond?

Here are some common pond creatures. Did you find any of them?

Water scorpions are not true scorpions but, with their long forelimbs and tail, they do look a bit scorpion-like. They can also sting but are not poisonous. Water scorpions are usually about 3–5 cm long and are often found moving slowly along at the bottom of the pond.

Mayfly nymphs are usually only found in clean water and will eventually grow into proper mayflies. The flies can be seen flying around in the spring – but they will only live for one day.

The **whirligig beetle** swims round and round in circles very fast when it is alarmed. Like the water spider, this beetle uses a bubble of air for diving and swimming underwater.

The dark brown **water spider** is a very good swimmer. It breathes by bringing air bubbles down from the surface and lives in an underwater silken nest, which is full of air bubbles.

Ramshorn snails are often found on water plants, because they eat the algae that grows on them. The snails are small, less than 1 cm across, with a flat coiled shell. Ramshorn snails are often eaten by fish.

Get that badge!

Identifying creatures in a pond, river, stream or rock pool could help you get a **Cub Scout Naturalist Activity Badge** and a **Cub Scout Scientist Activity Badge**.

Try to find out more about any other creatures you have found.

Pond pennies

A fun game of indoor pond dipping – just throw a penny to 'dip'.

You will need:
- two players or more
- a penny for each player
- paper and pen

How to play:
1. Lay your annual on the floor, or on a table, so that the pond game is as flat as possible.
2. Each player sits about 20–30 cm away from the game. The further away you sit, the more difficult it is to land your penny in the pond, so start off close and move further away as you play more games.
3. Take turns to gently toss your penny on to the pond. Where will it land? If your penny touches **any part** of a pond creature, you win points.
4. One person keeps score with the pen and paper. The first person to get ten points is the winner!

SCORING

5 points if it lands on a ramshorn snail

4 points if it lands on a water spider

3 points if it lands on a whirligig beetle

2 points if it lands on a mayfly nymph

1 point if it lands on a water scorpion

0 points if it lands in the pond, but does not touch a creature

BUT if your penny lands outside the pond, you lose one point!

Ben swims up

Ben had been thinking all week about the next Beaver Scout meeting. It was going to be his last – because Ben was going up to Cub Scouts. Hanging in his wardrobe was a smart new Cub uniform that he couldn't wait to wear. He felt a bit sad to be leaving behind some of the friends he had made in his Colony, but, as most of the Beaver Scouts would be joining Cubs later on, Ben would soon see them again.

There were three Beaver Scouts moving up together – Ben, Emily and Jack – so Ben didn't feel at all lonely. Cub Scouts sounded brilliant. They did similar things to Beavers, like playing games, earning badges and going on trips. But because Cubs were older they were allowed to do even more exciting things, like going on overnight camps in the woods! Ben had always wanted to do this.

Ben, Emily and Jack had even been to some Cub Scout meetings. The Cub Scout Leader was called Robert and he was very friendly. Robert had introduced them to all the Cubs and explained how Packs were divided up into groups of six. The leader of each group was called a Sixer. This was a very special responsibility. 'I wonder if I might be a Sixer one day?' thought Ben to himself.

Robert also told them all about a ceremony that would be held at their last Beaver meeting. It was called 'Swimming Up'.

'Do we need to bring our swimming costumes?' asked Jack.

'No, no!' laughed Robert. 'It's not real swimming. You just *pretend* to swim. There are lots of different ways to celebrate moving up to Cubs but this is our way of saying goodbye to the Beaver Colony and moving up into the Pack. I think you'll enjoy it.'

Ben, Emily and Jack looked at each other, smiling. It sounded like fun!

Finally the big day arrived. Ben had a very busy time at school. First there was assembly, then Ben's class had their weekly swimming lesson in the local pool. Ben was in the beginners' group. He had been using a float for a while, but this week his swimming instructor asked him to have a try without one.

'Put your goggles on, put your face in the water and try floating on your tummy,' she said. Ben had a bit of trouble at first but eventually mastered the art of floating with his face in the water, his arms and legs spread out like a starfish.

'Great – now kick your legs, push with your arms and try to move forward,' said the instructor encouragingly.

Ben did just that – and found that he was actually moving through the water! He was swimming! It was an incredible feeling.

By the end of the lesson Ben had swum a whole width of the pool. He felt *very* pleased with himself. 'I can't wait to tell Mum and Dad when they get home tonight!' thought Ben.

The day went quickly, and it was soon home time. Because Ben's parents were at work, Ben got picked up by his childminder, Janice. Janice's son, James, was a Beaver Scout too, though he was a bit younger than Ben.

Ben and James had tea, then got changed into their Beaver uniforms. Ben suddenly realized that this was the last time he would ever wear his blue sweatshirt. He looked at all the Activity Badges he had earned while at Beavers. He'd be so proud when he got his first Cub Scout Activity badge to show off on his green jumper!

The Beaver meeting was a lot of fun, as always. They played lots of games, and afterwards they had drinks and biscuits.

Soon the meeting came to an end and Ben felt a tingle of excitement – it was time for their special leaving ceremony! The Cub Scout meeting always took place straight after the Beaver meeting and that evening the Cub Scouts had arrived a few minutes early, to welcome the new members. They filed into the hall with their leader, Robert, all looking very smart.

'Emily, Jack and Ben – would you like to come and stand over here?' said the Beaver Scout leader, Brian. 'Tonight is a very special meeting for you, because you are leaving Beavers and moving on to Cubs. We will miss you – but we know you are going to have a brilliant time being Cub Scouts!'

Ben, Emily and Jack walked shyly over to Brian. Then Robert, the Cub Scout Pack Leader, spoke.

'Welcome to our Pack, Ben, Emily and Jack. We are really looking forward to having you with us and we know you are going to be a great addition to the Pack. Tonight we are going to ask you to swim across the river. This marks your journey from Beaver Scouts to Cub Scouts.'

Robert and Brian organized the Beaver Colony and the Cub Pack so that they were standing in two horseshoe shapes facing each other.

'Come forward, Sixers,' said Robert. Two boys and a girl stepped forward and shook hands with Emily, Ben and Jack, using the special Scout left handshake.

Then Brian shook hands with them. 'Goodbye Beavers and have fun,' he said. 'Now – you can swim, wade or jump across the river to join your new Cub Scout friends. Which will it be?'

'Swimming, please!' said Ben, excitedly. 'OK, off you go!' said Brian. Together the three Sixers and the three new Cubs 'swam' their way across the pretend river to the Cubs facing them. Ben did a nifty front crawl, Emily chose breast stroke while Jack – well – no one was quite sure what Jack was doing but it was certainly his own unique style!

When they reached the 'river bank', Robert shook their hands. 'Well done, Cub Scouts!' he said. 'Now you can call me Akela. Get ready for the Grand Howl! You can join in if you like.'

Ben, Emily and Jack had heard the Grand Howl before. They couldn't quite remember all the words but they joined in on the part that went 'A-ke-la – we'll do our best!' They felt like proper Cub Scouts now!

As the Howl came to an end, Ben looked up to see his mum and dad standing by the door. They must have arrived early to watch the ceremony – and he hadn't even noticed them.

'Mum, Dad!' shouted Ben and ran towards them. 'It's been the best day ever. I learned to swim – on the same day that I swam up to Cubs.'

'Well done, Ben!' His parents were delighted. 'If you keep on like this, your first Cub Scout badge might be for swimming,' said Mum, giving him a hug.

Ben's eyes were shining as he thought about all the new fun activities he'd soon be doing with his new Pack. 'Can we go swimming this weekend?' he asked excitedly. 'Well, how could we say no to our champion swimmer?' laughed his dad.

Brilliant badges

Earning a new badge is a great achievement. No wonder Cub Scouts everywhere wear their badges with pride.

There are so many different badges you can get when you become a Cub Scout. You start off with a **Membership Award** when you learn all about the section you are joining. Then there's a **Joining In Badge** which you can get every year for taking part in all the exciting activities and meetings. There are **Activity Badges** for 33 different skills, from martial arts to map reading, plus six **staged Activity Badges**. You can also try for special **Challenge Badges** which test your skill and determination – and if you really put your mind to it, you might earn **The Chief Scout's Silver Award**. This is the top award you can receive as a Cub Scout.

33 badges by nine!

When Rebecca Hooper from Norfolk was nine years old, she broke records when she became the youngest Cub Scout to get all 33 of the Cub Scout Activity Badges. Way to go, Rebecca!

Proud Rebecca learned many new skills in order to gain her badges. She:
- repaired a puncture on her bicycle
- made a computer desk for her DIY badge
- learned how to read a map
- sailed a boat.

But the badge that inspired her the most was the **Animal Carer Activity Badge** – because Rebecca now wants to become a vet when she is older.

Amazing Alex

Do you know anyone who has *all* the Cub Scout badges sewn on to his or her shirt? Meet Alex Edge from Caterham, who gained all 33 badges by the age of ten! This was an incredible achievement for Alex, as he is autistic and can find it hard to concentrate at times. But this didn't stop him designing and building a birdhouse for the DIY Badge and navigating a route by map from his house to Wembley Stadium!

Alex said: *'The best thing was the camping and canal boat trips and I am very pleased with what I have achieved.'* So you should be, Alex!

Answers on page 62.

Can you guess what these badges from 1956 are for?

Badges old and new

The whole idea of earning badges began at the first Scout Camp on Brownsea Island in 1907. Lord Baden-Powell (the founder of the Scouting Movement) gave each boy who took part his own special copper badge.

Since then many badges have been added to the Scout collection. Some of the earliest Scout badges no longer exist – among these are badges for Blacksmith, Bee-Master, Dairyman, Bookbinder and Miner. There was even a Master-at-Arms badge which included Boxing and Wrestling!

Nowadays, the most popular Cub Scout Activity Badges are the Nights Away and Hikes Away Staged Activity Badges. How many activity badges have you got?

'GETTING MY SWIMMER STAGED ACTIVITY BADGE PUSHED ME TO MY LIMITS – BUT I'M GLAD I DID IT.'

Ben (9)

The World Membership Badge

You are sure to have seen this emblem on your Membership Award and on other Scouting badges. It is called a Fleur-de-Lys (a lily). Lord Baden-Powell chose it for the Scouting Movement because the lily is a symbol of peace and purity.

There are several other important things that the Fleur-de-Lys represents for Scouts:

- The three tips of the flower remind us of the three points of the Scout Promise – Duty to God, Service to Others and Obedience to the Scout Law.
- The two stars stand for Knowledge and Truth.
- The ten points of the stars represent the ten points of the original Scout Law.
- The circle of rope represents the unity and family of the Scouts.
- The Fleur-de-Lys also reminded Baden-Powell of the north point used on maps (showing the true way to go).
- The reef knot – which cannot be undone when pulled – stands for strength.

'I'M DOING THE LOCAL KNOWLEDGE ACTIVITY BADGE AT THE MOMENT – IT'S REALLY INTERESTING, YOU FIND OUT THINGS ABOUT YOUR AREA THAT YOU WOULD NORMALLY NEVER KNOW.'

Alex (9)

Design your own badge

Have you got an idea for a new Cub Scout badge? Draw your design and write down what you would need to do to get this badge.

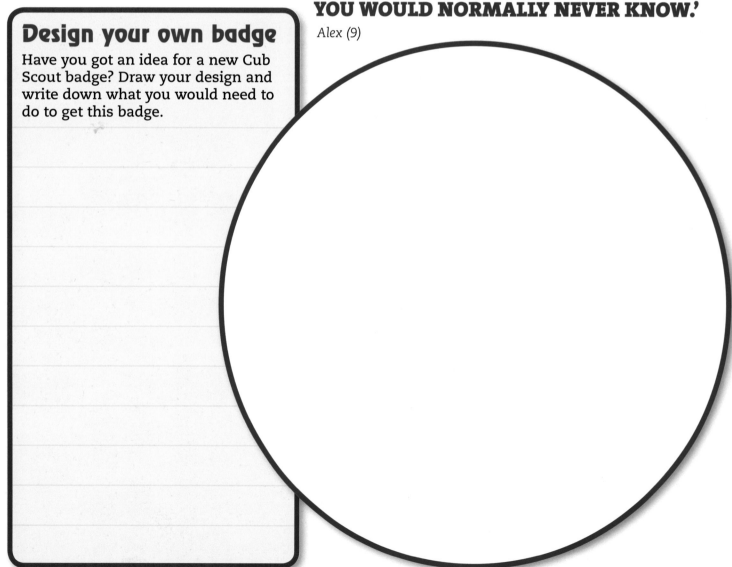

Badge brainteasers

How much do you know about the Cub Scout badges? Find out if you're a badge brainiac!

1 What shape are the Partnership Award badges?
a Circular
b Rectangular
c Triangular

2 On which arm does a Cub Scout wear his/her Cub Scout Activity Badges?
a Left
b Right
c Both

3 How many Joining In Badges can you gain during your time as a Cub Scout?

4 Can you name this badge?

5 There are six Challenge Badges. Can you fill in the missing letters of their names?

Pr_mise Challenge

Com_unity Challenge

F__ness Challenge

Creati__ Challenge

Gl_bal Challenge

Outd__r Challenge

6 Can you name the five Activity Badges below?

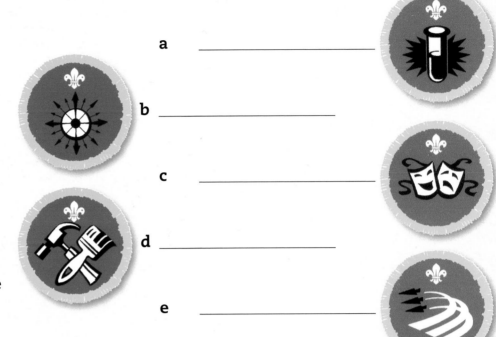

a _____

b _____

c _____

d _____

e _____

7 For which activity badges would you do the following tasks? Write the letters in the boxes.

- Look after a pet for at least three months
- Do a Sargent Jump
- Design and make a greetings card
- Show how to use the Green Cross Code
- Sew on a badge or button
- Know how to protect your home from fire
- Have a simple conversation in another language

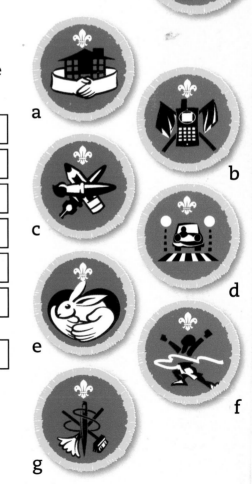

8 Which of these is *not* a Cub Scout Activity Badge?
a Chef
b Collector
c Climber

The great Atlantic challenge

It's the ultimate challenge – how would you do it?

The Atlantic Ocean is huge. It covers about one-fifth (20 per cent) of the Earth's surface.

Nowadays we can get on a plane and fly across this vast area of water in just a few hours, but it wasn't always this easy. Hundreds of years ago, explorers spent months at sea in rickety wooden sailing ships in their quest to reach the Americas.

The early twentieth century saw the age of the great ocean liner, when huge steamships filled with hundreds of passengers made the long Atlantic crossing. One of the most famous steamships was the *Titanic* – which hit an iceberg and sank in the North Atlantic on 15 April 1912.

Since those times, travelling has got much safer, easier and faster. Many thousands of people have now sailed or flown across the Atlantic – but none have done the journey quite like these intrepid adventurers!

Swimming Sensation

Ben Lecomte is no ordinary swimmer. In 1998 he became the first person to swim across the Atlantic! It took him 73 days, swimming for eight hours a day and resting on a sailing boat in between. Ben faced storms, winds, jellyfish – and sharks! He had to use a special machine called a POD (Protective Oceanic Device) which keeps sharks away with an electromagnetic field. And he's not finished with swimming challenges – Ben is currently training to swim across the Pacific Ocean!

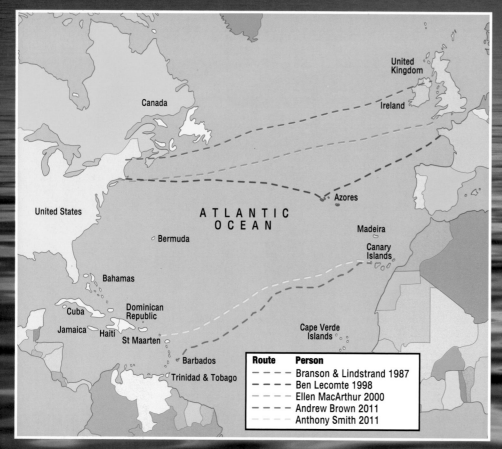

Route	Person
– – –	Branson & Lindstrand 1987
– ▪ –	Ben Lecomte 1998
– – –	Ellen MacArthur 2000
– – –	Andrew Brown 2011
– – –	Anthony Smith 2011

The dramatic rescue of the Virgin Atlantic Flyer's failed second attempt to circumnavigate the globe.

Rough Rowing

In 2011 Andrew Brown took part in a race called the Atlantic Challenge – also known as the world's toughest rowing race. Andrew rowed so fast that he broke the record for the fastest ever solo Atlantic crossing. The crossing, from the Canary Islands to Barbados, took him 40 days in a 5.7-metre rowing boat. The journey was very hard going and Andrew suffered from rashes, blisters and cramps. He also lost 19 kg in weight.

Up, Up and Away . . .

Adventurers Richard Branson (who was once a Scout himself) and Per Lindstrand made history in 1987 by becoming the first people to cross the Atlantic in a hot-air balloon. The balloon was specially made for the journey and was named the *Virgin*

Atlantic Flyer. The two men flew a distance of 4,920 kilometres and did the crossing in just under 32 hours! They landed in Ireland but had to bail out at the last minute, jumping into the sea. They were rescued by a helicopter.

In 1998 Branson and Lindstrand tried to fly round the world in a balloon – and had to be rescued again!

Andrew Brown nears the end of his exhausting trip

Sailing Solo

Dame Ellen MacArthur is well known for breaking sailing records. In 2000, Ellen sailed in the *Kingfisher* from Plymouth, UK, to Rhode Island, USA, in 14 days, 23 hours and 11 minutes. Ellen then went on to become the fastest person in the world to circumnavigate (go around) the world single-handedly in 2005.

Ellen knew she wanted to be a sailor from a young age – she even saved her school dinner money for eight years so that she could buy her first small boat!

Quick quiz

1 The Atlantic Ocean is the second largest of the five oceans in the world – can you name the other four oceans? Which is the largest?

2 If you put all five oceans in the world together, roughly how much of the Earth's surface would they cover?
   a 70 per cent
   b 50 per cent
   c 25 per cent

Answers on page 62.

Rafting Adventure

In 2011, Anthony Smith, along with three of his friends, decided to cross the Atlantic on a raft. Quite an unusual ambition for anyone – but Anthony was 85 years old! Their raft measured just 13 metres by 6 metres, had a mast and a sail and was named *An-Tiki*. The four men sailed a distance of more than 4,000 kilometres in 66 days. There were a few problems along the way – their rudder broke after only two days at sea – but they fixed it and completed their challenge to lots of cheers.

Get that badge!

Taking part in sailing, boating, rafting or rowing activities can help you get your **Cub Scout Water Activities Activity Badge**.

Tips for a transatlantic crossing

- Even though you are surrounded by water, you can't drink it – sea water is too salty! You need to take lots of fresh drinking water to survive.
- You'll also need plenty of nutritious food – especially if you're doing lots of physical work, like rowing.
- It can take a very long time to cross this ocean, depending on your mode of transport. Could you cope with being completely on your own at sea for weeks at a time, like Ellen MacArthur?
- You'll need lots of training before you attempt the crossing – it can take years to prepare. You also need to be ready if things go wrong. Bad weather and equipment problems are common.

Make a paper boat

Try your hand at making this fun origami boat – then see if it floats!

You will need:

- A rectangular-shaped piece of paper – the bigger the paper, the bigger the boat. Standard A4 paper is fine.
- Your hands!
- Crayons – optional
- Toothpick, paper flag, glue – optional

How to do it:

1 If you want your boat to be nice and bright, colour all over one side of the paper. Using crayons is a good idea because they are made of wax and help to repel water – making your finished boat a little more waterproof.

2 Fold the paper in half. The coloured side should be inwards.

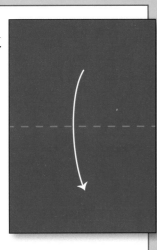

3 From the folded edge, fold the two corners down so that they meet in the middle, like two triangles.

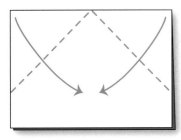

4 Fold the bottom part of the paper upwards. Turn it over and do the same on the other side. You will now have a paper hat shape.

5 Pull your hat apart and squash it down into a diamond shape. As you do so, tuck the flaps underneath each other to make a neat shape. Press the creases well.

6 Now take hold of the bottom corner of your diamond (the open end) and bring it upwards. Do the same on the other side and you end up with a triangle.

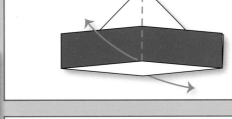

7 Open up the triangle and squash it into a smaller diamond shape.

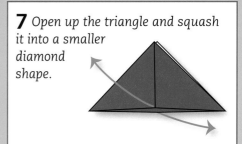

8 Take two corners at the point of the diamond (the only ones you can pull apart) and gently pull them apart to make your boat. Once it is opened, you will need to press down inside the boat to flatten down the 'decks' and help the sail stand up straight.

9 You can add a nautical flag by inserting a toothpick into the centre of the sail and sticking on a little paper triangle.
Now you can sail your boat in a sink or bath. Yo ho ho!

If you like blowing bubbles try these great ideas for bubbletastic fun!

Brilliant bubbles

Bubbles are beautiful to watch and fun to make. But how do they happen?

The science of bubbles

A bubble is simply air trapped inside a thin 'skin' of soapy water. Water is made up of millions of tiny droplets called molecules – so small that they can only be seen with a microscope. These water molecules are attracted to each other. When they stick together on the surface of water the molecules produce what's called 'surface tension' – and this is what helps make bubbles.

If you've ever seen a small insect called a pond skater 'walking' on the water, you'll already have witnessed surface tension in action.

When you blow air into a bubble, you are stretching the water molecules into a sphere (a perfectly round shape, like a ball). But there's one very important extra ingredient – soap. Adding detergent or washing-up liquid to the water lets the skin of the bubble become elastic and stretch, to hold the air without bursting. You can also blow bigger bubbles, without them popping!

Making brilliant bubbles

Start off by making your own bubble mixture:

Bubble mixture

You will need:
- Washing-up liquid
- Water
- Glycerine (available from most chemists)
- Large wide bowl or deep sided tray
- Tablespoon
- Plastic cup for measuring

How to do it:

1 Pour one cup of washing-up liquid and two cups of water into the bowl and mix.

2 Add four tablespoonfuls of glycerine and mix again. Glycerine will help make your bubbles even stronger.

3 Let's blow some bubbles! There are lots of things that you can use to blow bubbles – try string, straws, plastic bottles or plates. For the biggest bubbles you will need to blow very slowly and gently, otherwise they will pop!

Straw bubbles

You will need:
- A plastic straw
- Small scissors

How to do it:

1 Bend the straw into a square or a triangular shape (it won't be perfect, but that's part of the fun). Carefully cut three small slits into one end of the straw and gently push it inside the other end to complete your shape.

2 Now dip the blower in the solution and blow a bubble – what shape do you think the bubble will be?

3 You'll soon discover that whatever shape your blower is, your bubble will always be round. This is because when you blow air into the bubble, the

stretchy 'skin' around it tries to take up the least amount of space it can – and a round shape takes up less space than a square shape.

If you ever do make a square or triangular bubble, please let us know!

Giant bottle bubbles

You will need:
- A clean plastic water or fizzy pop bottle – small or large.
- Sharp scissors and a grown-up helper

How to do it:

1 Ask your grown-up helper to cut off the bottom of the plastic bottle, leaving as smooth an edge as possible. **This is slippery to cut so do not try it yourself.**

2 Dip the open end of your bottle blower into the bubble mixture – shake it gently so that it isn't dripping too much.

3 Now gently blow. With a bit of practice you should be able to blow impressively large bubbles!

Plate bubbles

You will need:
- Sharp scissors and a grown-up helper
- A plastic plate

How to do it:

1 Ask your helper to cut the centre of the plate out carefully, starting in the middle of the plate. You should be left with a plastic ring.

2 Dip the ring into the bubble solution and blow yourself a nice big bubble!

The mysterious moon

The moon is one of the closest objects in the solar system to our planet – but how much do you know about it?

Have you ever looked up into the night sky, watched the moon glowing brightly among the stars and wondered what it might be like up there?

Humans throughout history have found the moon mysterious and beautiful. Many have worshipped it. In Roman times they called their moon goddess Luna – the Latin word for 'moon'. Today, we use the word 'lunar' to describe anything to do with the moon.

But it wasn't until July 1969 that a human actually landed on the moon.

Get that badge!

Finding out about the moon and presenting the information can help you get a **Cub Scout Astronomer Activity Badge**.

Moon landing!

Around the world, millions of excited people watched on TV as a piece of history was made by the NASA Apollo 11 mission. The man who first stepped on to the moon's dusty surface was an American astronaut called Neil Armstrong, followed by his colleague, Buzz Aldrin. The two astronauts had travelled in a small lunar module called *Eagle* for the final part of the journey. They made their landing on a part of the moon called The Sea of Tranquility.

They stayed on the moon for 21½ hours and collected lots of rock samples, which have given us most of our knowledge of the moon.

Moon myths

Not everything you hear about the moon is true!

The moon is made of green cheese
Not true! The moon is made mainly of rock, though not the same rock as you find on Earth. On its surface is a layer of fine dust and rocky debris called

Both Buzz Aldrin and Neil Armstrong were once Scouts.

'regolith'. The moon's surface is full of craters, made by comets and asteroids which have collided with it.

There is a man living on the moon
It's fascinating to think that there might something or someone living on the moon. But we haven't been able to find anything living there. Scientists don't think the conditions are right for life on our moon but they are looking at other moons, such as Europa (Jupiter's moon), for possible alien life.

The phases of the moon

We can only see the moon because its surface reflects light from the Sun. Because the moon constantly orbits the Earth, it looks different depending on its position. Sometimes it looks like a crescent shape, at other times it is full and round – and sometimes you can't see it at all!

The shape of the bright part of the moon that we can see from Earth is called a 'phase'. It takes the Moon roughly 29 days to go through all eight phases.

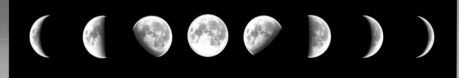

The eight phases of the moon that can be seen from the Northern Hemisphere.

41

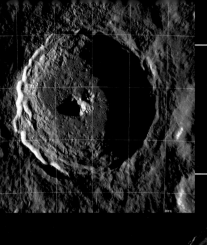

Moon craters: did you know?

The surface of the moon is covered in hundreds of craters of different sizes. They were made by objects, such as meteorites and comets, hitting the moon. Many of these craters have been named – just a few of them are shown on the map.

ARISTOTELES

ARISTARCHUS

PICARD

PLINIUS

SEA OF TRANQUILITY

COPERNICUS

LANGRENUS

ALBATEGNIUS

THEOPHILUS

VENDELINUS

PICCOLOMINI

PITATUS

JANSSEN

SCHICKARD

STÖFLER

TYCHO

Moon-watching

The moon is the easiest thing to observe in the night sky because it is relatively close to Earth compared with the other planets and stars. If you have a pair of binoculars or a telescope, you can look in more detail at the moon's surface and see its many craters. See if you can spot any of the features shown on our moon map. Start off with:

The Tycho Crater

The Tycho Crater is near the moon's South Pole. It measures about 85 kilometres across and it is one of the most visible craters on the moon surface, appearing as a bright spot. You might even be able to see it without a telescope.

The Sea of Tranquility

The place where the lunar module made its historic landing is not actually a sea at all – it's a large basin-like dip on the moon's surface.

WARNING: NEVER look at the sky with binoculars or a telescope during daylight hours!

Moon mirth

When isn't the moon hungry? When it's full.

What's an astronaut's favourite day of the week? Moonday.

How does the man in the moon get his hair cut? Eclipse it.

What did one alien say to the other? 'Pleased to meteor!'

How do you organize a space party? You planet!

What's big, bright and really stupid? A fool moon!

What holds up the moon? Moonbeams.

What's the best game to play in space? Moonopoly.

Where do astronauts keep their sandwiches? In a launch box.

Fun food art

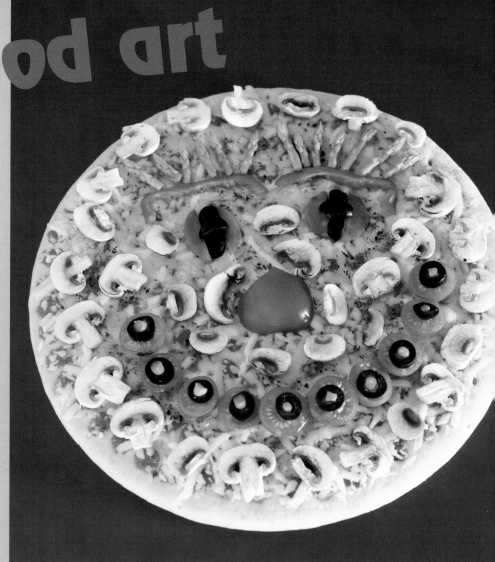

Make your snacks look as pretty as a picture with these great ideas. All you need is some food, a grown-up helper and *a lot* of imagination.

Pizza people

Why make do with an ordinary pizza when you can create a pizza person?

Use plain cheese and tomato pizzas (or make your own). For a smaller version, use sliced English muffins. Grill with grated cheese on top.

Get artistic with some fresh ingredients for the toppings. Try: ham, mushroom, pepperoni, peppers, onions, sweetcorn, cooked peas, tomato, lettuce, celery, olives and pineapple.

Create a variety of faces with different expressions and have lots of fun with the hair!

Tasty creatures

Make everyday sandwiches and salads into your favourite pets, animals and insects. Try making a ladybird out of a whole tomato cut into pieces. Use cream cheese to stick the bits together, olives for the spots, chives for the antennae and salad ingredients for the base.

Create a menagerie of animals by slicing sandwiches and rolls and using pieces of fruit, vegetable and salad to bring your creature to life!

44

Fruit 'n' veg art

Use delicious healthy fruit and vegetables to make all kinds of pictures. Let your imagination run wild! Here are some ideas for inspiration.

Freaky fruity faces

For a fun dessert you can make individual fruit faces on small plates – great for party guests.

Use two slices of kiwi fruit for the eyes with orange or apple slices above them for eyebrows. Place a blueberry or a raspberry in the centre of each eye for the pupil.

Slice the end from a banana and place it on the plate so that it sticks up like a nose.

Finally, a curved piece of melon makes a great mouth – you could even carve some teeth into it!

Why not give everyone a plate and a time limit to make up their very own freaky face? Award 'prizes' for the silliest face, the scariest face, and the one that looks most like someone in your Pack!

The prizes are . . . gobbling up your fruity face!

Tip – if you're using sliced bananas, toss them in a little lemon juice to stop the pieces going brown.

The art of food

Making art out of food is nothing new. Giuseppe Arcimboldo was a sixteenth-century Italian artist. He painted portraits of imaginary people made out of fruit and vegetables! What do you think?

Flower power

Flowers not only look beautiful – they are an essential part of a plant's life cycle.

If you enjoy seeing flowers growing in parks, gardens and woods, you'll be interested to know that there's more to those pretty petals than meets the eye.

Why are flowers so brightly coloured?

They want to get attention! Plants need to attract insects and other creatures to help with a process called pollination. Pollination makes the seeds to grow new plants.

Why are bees and insects so important to flowers?

An insect, such as a bee, lands on a flower and sips nectar from it. Pollen from the flower sticks to its body and when the bee flies away, it transfers the pollen to the next flower it visits. That's pollination!

Flowery facts

- Many insects, such as ants, beetles, butterflies and moths, pollinate plants. But honeybees are especially good at it – nearly 80 per cent of all crop pollination is down to bees. Plants can also be pollinated by birds, the wind – and some plants even pollinate themselves.
- There are roughly 250,000 different types of flowering plant in the world.
- Different creatures have their own favourite flowers. Bees are attracted to bright blue and purple. Butterflies like yellow, orange, pink and red flowers, while hummingbirds prefer red, pink and purple petals.

Stunning sunflowers

Tall and yellow, bright and blooming, sunflowers are a beautiful sight. Would you like to grow one? Here's how:

You will need:
- A packet of sunflower seeds
- Flower pots or washed yogurt pots
- Compost

How to do it:
1 The best time to plant your seeds is in the spring – mid-March is ideal. You can start growing the sunflowers inside in a light place as this will help prevent frost damaging them or animals digging them up.

2 Water regularly until shoots start to appear in two or three weeks' time.

3 Once the plants are about 10 cm tall, you can plant them in the garden or in an outdoor container. Choose a sunny spot – sunflowers love lots of sunlight. They also like damp soil so water them regularly in the evenings.

4 Watch them grow – and enjoy their beautiful yellow sun-shaped flowers. Many sunflowers will grow to between one and three metres tall! If your sunflowers begin to droop and bend over, you can tie them to a cane with string.

5 In autumn the flower heads will fade and you can harvest the sunflower seeds. Cut the heads off at the stem and tie the heads together, hanging them upside down in a warm, dry place for two weeks. Then you can rub the face of the flower to release the seeds inside.

Things to do with sunflower seeds
- Save them in an envelope. Put in a cool, dry place and plant them next spring.
- Scatter them on a bird table for a tasty snack the birds will love.
- Eat them! Ask a grown-up to help you roast the seeds on a tray in the oven until they are crisp and brown. You can add a shake of salt afterwards too.

Get that badge!

Identifying wild flowers can help you get your **Cub Scout Naturalist Activity Badge**. Collecting seeds from plants and finding out about their life cycle can help you get a **Cub Scout Scientist Activity Badge**.

My favourite flower

What's your favourite flower? Draw and colour it here.

Get on your bike!

Have fun, get fit and have a 'wheely' good time!

Cycling is brilliant fun and everyone can do it. So, if you're lucky enough to own a bike, make the most of it by getting out and about with your friends and family. Make sure you get the best out of your bike by knowing how to look after it.

The best places to cycle are in parks and recreation grounds or on cycle trails or bike paths that are well away from busy roads. You might even be lucky enough to live near an adventure playground or BMX track.

Bikes for everyone

Bikes, like people, come in all shapes and sizes. Here are some designs that you might have seen before – and some you probably haven't . . .

BMX or Bicycle Motocross started in the United States in the 1970s when fans began modifying their bikes to do stunts, tricks and jumps. A BMX bike has a strong frame designed for fast cycling on a smooth surface. It needs to cope with large and small jumps on and off ramps so it usually has smaller wheels than a mountain bike, a single gear and no suspension. Helmets, gloves, knee and elbow pads are essential for this nerve-racking sport!

Mountain bikes – these are bikes made for off-road cycling. They are chunkier than standard bikes with wider wheels and knobbly tyres – perfect for coping with bumpy surfaces in woods and on rocky trails. Mountain bikes usually have lots of gears for all the different kinds of terrain which might face the mountain-bike rider.

Recumbent bikes – to ride this bike, you need to lie down! The recumbent rider sits much lower down, lying back with his/her weight spread out over a larger area. These bikes feel different to standard bikes and take a little getting used to – but because of their streamlined design, they can go faster. The world speed record for a bike is currently held by a recumbent.

Tandem bikes – ever fancied trying a bicycle made for two? Tandems are bikes designed for two or more people to ride. You get double the pedalling power but you need to work as a team – making sure that you start and stop at the same times!

Cycling in the past

Early bikes were much more difficult to ride than today's models. In 1865 the first cycles were made of wood and called 'boneshakers' – as they literally shook your bones when riding down cobbled streets!

In 1870 a new design appeared. Called the high wheel bicycle, it was nicknamed the 'penny-farthing' because of its unusual shape. It had one large and one very small wheel. The cyclist sat high up above the large wheel, probably hoping that he/she wouldn't fall off! Do you think you could have ridden one?

The ABC of bike maintenance

Your bike should last you for a long time if you look after it well. Here are the things you should do regularly.

A is for AIR

Keep tyres pumped up – before you go on a bike ride, pinch your tyres to check that they are fully inflated. Find out how to repair a puncture and get yourself a puncture kit – it can come in very useful!

B is for BRAKES

It's very important to be able to stop when you need to. Test each brake – front and back – regularly. If you have to press very hard on your brake levers to stop the bike, your brake pads probably need replacing.

C is for CHAIN

Take a look at your bike chain and make sure it isn't loose or hanging off. Oil it with bicycle brake oil (but not too much) every few months. This will keep the chain running smoothly and will make pedalling easier.

Bicycle know-how

Do you know all the parts of a bicycle? Can you fill in the missing names?

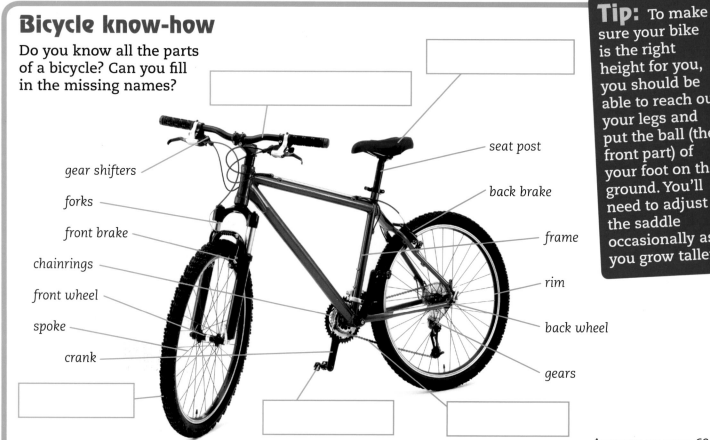

gear shifters

forks

front brake

chainrings

front wheel

spoke

crank

seat post

back brake

frame

rim

back wheel

gears

Tip: To make sure your bike is the right height for you, you should be able to reach out your legs and put the ball (the front part) of your foot on the ground. You'll need to adjust the saddle occasionally as you grow taller!

Answers on page 62.

Jason Lewis with his pedal-powered boat, Moksha.

Keeping safe on your bike

- **Always wear a helmet.** You'll need one that fits you well and isn't loose.
- **Get seen.** Wear bright or fluorescent colours that drivers, pedestrians and other cyclists can easily spot. If you must ride at night you need working lights and reflectors on your bike.
- **Dress sensibly.** Wear well-fitting shoes that really grip the pedals – not flip-flops. Also wear close-fitting trousers that don't flap around and get caught in the chain.
- **Be aware.** Look at your surroundings and spot potential hazards such as potholes, gravel, puddles and leaves – *before* you come off your bike! Use your bell to let people know you are cycling up behind them.
- **What's your Bikeability?** If you would like to get more confident on your bike, why not do a Bikeability Test? Your school will probably be able to organize this, or you can look at their website to find out more details.

  During Level 1 training, you will learn to control your bike and gain basic skills, including starting and pedalling; stopping; manoeuvring; signalling, and using the gears on your bike.

Pedal Power!

When adventurer Jason Lewis decided to take a trip around the world in 1994 he thought he would set himself a challenge – to do the journey using only his own muscle power. So Jason cycled, walked and rollerbladed on land, and used a pedal boat and kayak on the water. During his journey, he broke his leg, got attacked by a crocodile and caught malaria – but eventually became the only person to have circumnavigated the globe *without* motors or sails. So, how long did the journey take him? 4,833 days – or 13 years.

Get that badge!

Owning a bike and helmet and keeping your bike in good condition can help you get a **Cub Scout Cyclist Activity Badge**.

Cycling champions

How did some of our champions get started?

In August 2012 Sir Chris Hoy became Britain's greatest Olympian when he won his sixth gold Olympic medal. Chris first got interested in cycling when he saw the film E.T. as a boy. It has a famous scene in which a boy and an alien (E.T.) cycle through the sky on a BMX bike. After that he got hooked on BMX – which led to even greater things! Olympic gold medallist and nine-times world champion Victoria Pendleton took part in her first race at the age of nine – a 400-metre race on grass. As a young girl and teenager, she spent most of her spare time cycling with her dad.

Sir Chris Hoy and Victoria Pendleton: proud Olympic champions at the 2012 Olympic Games.

51

All-action Cubs!

Cub Scouts love being outdoors and trying new activities. Which of these fun-filled outdoor activities have you done before? Which ones would you like to do? Tick the boxes.

Climbing

Whether you go up a climbing wall or a mountain, you will feel great when you've reached the top!

Done it! Want to try it!

Archery

Shoot a bow and arrow, 'Robin Hood' style.

Done it! Want to try it!

Done it! Want to try it!

Zipwiring

Sometimes called Aerial Runway, you will shoot off down a rope or wire at speed. Whee!

Done it! Want to try it!

Karting

Race your friends around a track on a speedy go-kart!

Done it! Want to try it!

Zorbing

Roll around in a giant inflatable ball – on land or on water. It's brilliant fun!

Abseiling

'Walk' down the face of a wall or mountain with a harness on, controlling your speed as you go.

Done it! Want to try it!

Done it! Want to try it!

Orienteering

Use your map-reading skills – and your legs – to find a secret location. First there wins!

Canoeing

Have fun on the water and paddle yourself along on a canoe.

Done it! Want to try it!

Done it! Want to try it!

Pony trekking

Learn how to ride a pony and enjoy the outdoors at the same time.

Done it! Want to try it!

Crate climbing

Make a tower of crates and get all the way to the top! 'Crate' fun!

My top three outdoor activities

What do you enjoy doing the most when you're outdoors?

1

2

3

Why do WASPS sting?

There's nothing more annoying than being pestered by wasps when you're having a picnic!

Most people find wasps pretty irritating – and some make a *big* fuss when there's a wasp around! But wasps and bees don't usually go out of their way to attack humans. They sting only in self-defence or if they've been annoyed in some way.

Wasps are attracted to food, especially sweet drinks, and people have sometimes been stung while they are eating or drinking because they haven't noticed a wasp landing on their food or in their drink. Bees and wasps may also sting if you go too close to their hive – again, this is a form of defence.

Wasp know-how

The most common type of wasp has yellow and black stripes. But there many other colours, shapes and sizes – there is even a wasp which is red and green!

- Wasps live in nests of up to 10,000 workers. Nests are often found in places such as garden sheds or the lofts of houses.
- Wasps are amazing architects, making their nests from chewed-up wood.
- Wasps become more of a nuisance to humans in late summer when their normal food sources dry up and they start looking elsewhere.
- Wasps can sting several times – while bees can only sting once. But the amount of venom in a wasp sting is much less than that of a bee.

BUZZ OFF!

Keeping out of wasps' way

While there's no foolproof way to avoid being stung, there are a few ways to make it less likely:

- If pestered by a wasp or bee, move out of the way slowly and calmly. Waving your arms around and shouting will annoy it and make it more likely to sting.

- Be extra careful if you are eating or drinking (especially sweet things) outside. Check your drinking glasses and cans if there are wasps around.
- Wearing long sleeves, long trousers, socks and shoes can help protect you from stings.
- If you spot a bees' or wasps' nest when you are out and about, leave it well alone and move to another area.

If you are unlucky enough to be stung by a wasp you will be left with a sore, red and itchy area around the sting, which will last for a few days. The best thing to do is to wash the bite with soap and water, then cool off the skin with ice cubes or an ice-pack that has been wrapped in a cloth. You can also use special insect bite cream on the affected area.

If you have been stung by a bee it will have left behind a tiny venom sac in the skin. This needs to be removed as quickly as possible, as the sac can carry on pumping venom for about a minute. If possible, get a grown-up to help. The stinger can be pulled or pinched out with the fingers, with tweezers or with the edge of a bank card.

Wonderful wasps

Some people think that wasps are just annoying insects that have no useful function. But they'd be wrong. Wasps are very important to the food chain. They eat creatures such as spiders, caterpillars, ants and flies, helping to limit their numbers. This is a great help to farmers and gardeners as wasps kill a large number of the insects that can destroy crops.

Wasps provide food for other creatures too – many types of bird and dragonfly find wasps a tasty snack. And did you know that badgers are the main predator of wasps in Great Britain? Badgers dig up wasp's nests in order to find and eat the lovely juicy wasp grubs! Luckily, their thick hairy coats provide some protection against wasp stings.

Wasps collect honeydew, which helps plants pollinate. So wasps are both pest controllers and pollinators!

Wasps make papery nests in quiet, high places like attics or trees

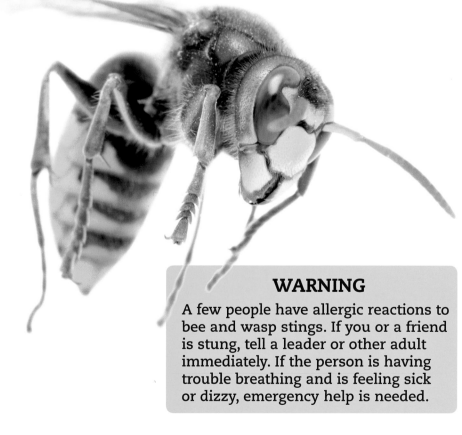

WARNING

A few people have allergic reactions to bee and wasp stings. If you or a friend is stung, tell a leader or other adult immediately. If the person is having trouble breathing and is feeling sick or dizzy, emergency help is needed.

55

Insect funnies

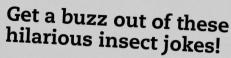

Why were the flies playing football in a saucer?
They were playing for the cup!

What do insects learn at school?
Mothematics.

Cub Scout: Ow, I've been stung by a wasp!
Cub leader: Let's put some cream on it.
Cub Scout: But it will be miles away by now!

What did the bee say to the flower?
'Hello, honey.'

Why do bees hum?
Because they've forgotten the words.

What goes hum-choo, hum-choo?
A bee with a cold.

How do you start an insect race?
One, two, flea – go!

What do you call an ant that lives with your great-uncle?
A great ant!

What has six legs, bites and talks in code?
A Morse-quito.

Why did the insect get told to leave the park?
Because it was a litterbug.

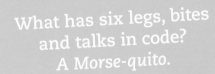

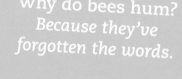

Bizarre body tricks

How NOT to perform the heavy-hand trick!

Sometimes your body can really play tricks on you. Try these fun experiments and see what happens!

Falling through the floor

Lie down on the floor and close your eyes. Ask a friend to gently lift up your legs and hold them in the air. Relax for about two minutes. Then your friend should lower your feet slowly to the ground. It'll feel like your legs are going through the floor!

Impossible letters

You'll need two pieces of scrap paper and two pens or pencils. Can you draw a big 'C' on one piece of paper with your left hand and a big 'U' on the other piece with your right hand? Now – can you write both letters with both hands at the same time?

Heavy hand

You will need two people for this trick. One person sits in a chair and places his/her right hand flat on top of his/her head. The other person stands up and tries to lift up the hand. Can it be done?

Pick-up problem

Stand against a wall with a small object like a matchbox directly in front of you on the floor. You must pick up the matchbox *without* bending your knees. Can you do it?

Floating arms

Stand in a doorway with the *back* of your hands pressed on each side of the door frame. Press against the frame, pushing outward as hard as you can, for at least 30 seconds. Now step out of the doorway and relax, letting your arms hang down loosely at your side. Your arms will try to rise upward at your side. Weird!

The big quiz

Find out how much you know from this year's Cub Scout Annual by giving our Big Quiz a try. If you're stuck, you can find all the answers by looking back through the book. Or just have a guess!

1 Which of these beetles would you usually find in a pond?

a Deathwatch beetle ☐

b Stag beetle ☐

c Whirligig beetle ☐

2 Where in the universe would you find The Sea of Tranquility?

a The Earth ☐

b The Moon ☐

c The Sun ☐

3 How many Olympic gold medals has Sir Chris Hoy won?

☐

4 Which of these creatures pollinates flowers and plants? The answer could be one or more of the following.

a Beetle ☐

b Butterfly ☐

c Honey bee ☐

5 Which is the largest ocean in the world?

a The Atlantic Ocean ☐

b The Pacific Ocean ☐

c The Indian Ocean ☐

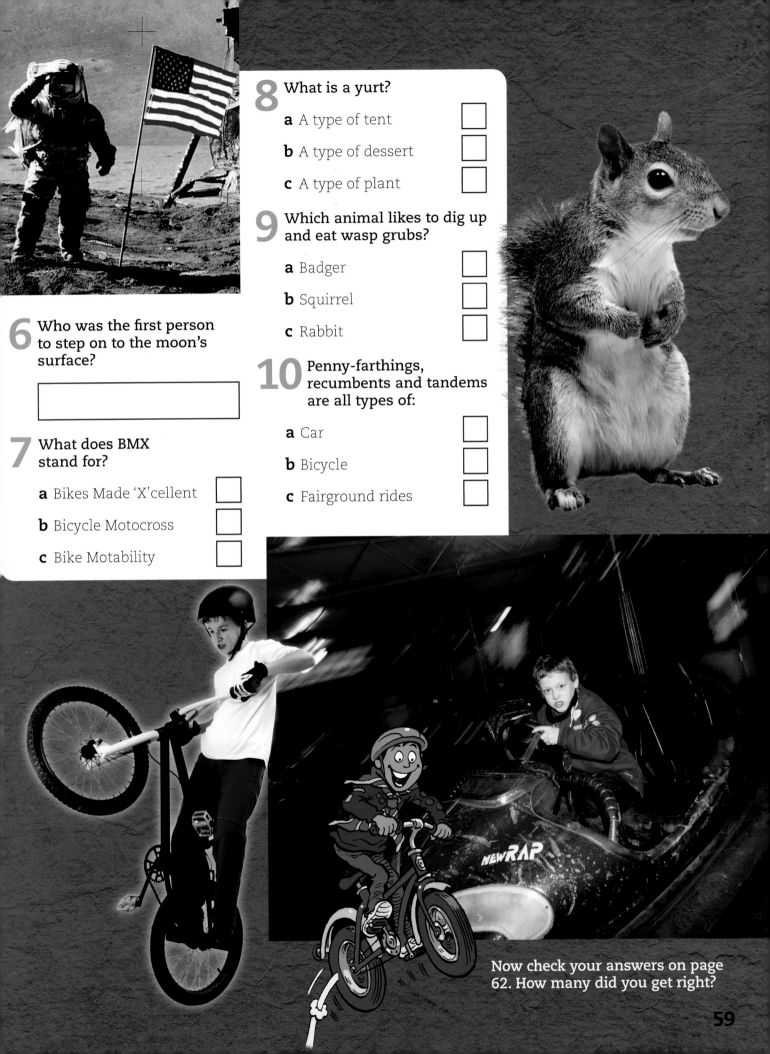

8 What is a yurt?

a A type of tent ☐

b A type of dessert ☐

c A type of plant ☐

9 Which animal likes to dig up and eat wasp grubs?

a Badger ☐

b Squirrel ☐

c Rabbit ☐

6 Who was the first person to step on to the moon's surface?

☐

10 Penny-farthings, recumbents and tandems are all types of:

a Car ☐

b Bicycle ☐

c Fairground rides ☐

7 What does BMX stand for?

a Bikes Made 'X'cellent ☐

b Bicycle Motocross ☐

c Bike Motability ☐

Now check your answers on page 62. How many did you get right?

Win a Cub Scout day out!

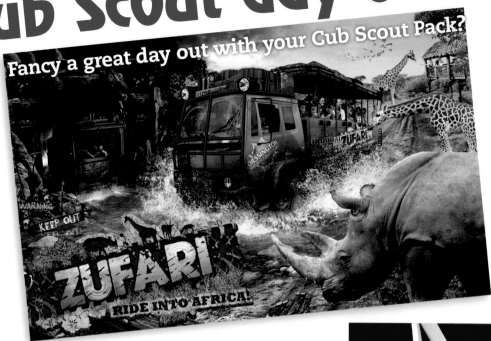

Fancy a great day out with your Cub Scout Pack?

ZUFARI RIDE INTO AFRICA!

Enter our competition and you could win an amazing day trip for 30 Cub Scouts plus 10 leaders to one of the UK's Top Attractions, thanks to Merlin Groups!

Just answer our question and you could be riding a rollercoaster, taking a safari adventure or coming face to face with sharks! The winner can choose to visit any one of the following top attractions:

- Alton Towers Resort
- Chessington World of Adventures Resort
- LEGOLAND® Windsor Resort
- THORPE PARK
- Madame Tussauds London or Blackpool
- SEA LIFE centres & Sanctuaries
- The Dungeons
- Warwick Castle
- LEGOLAND ® Discovery Centre Manchester
- Weymouth SEA LIFE Adventure Park and Tower
- The Blackpool Tower Attractions

To enter, just answer the following question: *Which continent does the new ZUFARI ride at Chessington World of Adventures Resort take you through?*

As a tie breaker, please also tell us in 50 words or fewer: *If you could take your Cub Scout Pack anywhere in the world – where would you go and why?*

Please email your answer to **communications@scouts.org.uk** or put your answers on a postcard and send them to:
**Cub Scout Annual 2014 Competition
The Scout Association,
Gilwell Park, Chingford
London E4 7QW**

The closing date for entries is **31 March 2014.** Good luck!
For full competition terms and conditions, please visit: http://www.merlingroups.com/misc/legal.aspx

Information for leaders

Merlin Groups is part of The Merlin Entertainments Group offering group savings and benefits at 28 of the UK's Top Attractions.

Scouts can benefit from savings of up to 75% off entry, FREE leader places and FREE familiarization tickets, as well as having the opportunity to work towards badge clauses whilst visiting.

Let your group escape into a whole new adventure; we now offer camping experiences at the Alton Towers Resort, Chessington World of Adventures Resort and Warwick Castle & sleepover experiences at some of the Blackpool Tower Attractions.

To find out about all our latest news and offers sign up to our newsletter at **www.merlingroups.com**

You can also like us on Facebook by visiting **www.facebook.com/MerlinGroups** or follow us on Twitter by visiting **www.twitter.com/Merlin_Groups**

Booking and advice
For further information and to book your day out visit **www.merlingroups.com/scouts** or call 0871 222 6944.

LEGO, the LEGO logo and LEGOLAND are trademarks of the LEGO Group. © 2013 The LEGO Group.

MERLIN GROUPS

Who won last year's competition?

Congratulations to Aengus, from 1st Stretford (Longford) Cubs, who won a fantastic trip to a Merlin Entertainments' Attraction for him and his Pack. He correctly identified that The Blackpool Tower is 158 metres tall.

Aengus told us all about why he loves being a Cub Scout:

'Firstly, Cubs is so revolutionary that as soon as the clock pings six I'm like, "Mum, Cubs is on, quick, let's grab the bikes and go!" and Mum's like, "Aengus, it doesn't start for an hour!" We also get to do awesome stuff like camping. That's why it's ace.'

Well done, Aengus!

CUBS Annual 2014
Packed with skills, stories and outdoor fun for cub scouts!

Join Scouting

Did you know that 400,000 boys and girls across the UK enjoy the challenge and adventure of Scouting? Anyone aged 6–25 can join the Scouts and take part in exciting activities from abseiling to zorbing. Scouting is about fun, friendship and welcoming everyone, whatever their background, faith or culture. Why not come and join the adventure?

Brilliant Beavers

Beaver Scouts are boys and girls aged between 6 and 8 years. They meet up regularly and play games, learn about the outdoors and earn all kinds of brilliant badges. If you're interested in becoming a Beaver Scout, find out where your local Colony meets and ask if you can go along one evening. If you enjoy yourself, you can find out how to become a member from the group leaders.

Cracking Cubs

Beavers go on to become **Cub Scouts,** who are aged 8–10½. You can join Cub Scouts in the six months leading up to your eighth birthday. At Cubs you can look forward to doing all the things that you did as a Beaver but with even more camps, interesting visits and outdoor fun. And badges, of course!

Super Scouts

Scouts are 10½ to 14 years old. They still meet up, play games and make the same Scout sign. But, as they are now older and part of a Scout Troop, they can take part in even more exciting activities such as Patrol projects, pioneering and longer camping expeditions. There is almost no limit to the fascinating and fun things you can do when you're a Scout!

FIND OUT MORE

For more information about Scouting and all the different badges and awards that Beaver Scouts, Cub Scouts and Scouts can gain, go to www.scouts.org.uk

Download My Badges – The Scout Association's Official Badge app for iPhone and iPod Touch, available now on iTunes and on Google Play for Android devices.

Download The Scouts: Secret Island Adventure – an exciting multi-level adventure game, including several mini arcade games, to test your hang-gliding, canoeing and mountain-boarding skills. Available on iTunes for iPhone, iPad, iPod Touch and on Google Play for Android devices.

Answers

Page 11: Camp Crisis.

- The gate into the field has been left open and the cows could get out.
- The flagpole is broken and is in danger of falling down.
- The campfire is too close to the tents – they could catch fire. There is an overhanging branch above the fire, which could also burn.
- A knife has been left sticking over the edge of the camping table – someone might get injured.
- The dirty dishes and cutlery are in a pile on the ground and there are flies buzzing around them. Someone could trip over them and it is also unhygienic.
- A box of matches has been left open and there are matches scattered around – they could cause a fire.
- Clothes, shoes and bags are strewn around the site and someone could trip over them.
- The first-aid box is empty. If someone needs first aid, there is nothing to use.
- The children should not be playing football in a field where there are animals.
- There is no grown-up or Camp Leader supervising the children.

Page 14: Puzzling food.
Fruit Sudoku: see right. Greedy Grid: sou**P/P**ea, chees**E/E**gg, past**A/A**pple, flou**R/R**ice – the campfire snack is **PEAR**. Sizzling Search: see right.

Page 31: Brilliant badges.
Top to bottom: Air Spotter, Athlete, Gardener, Handyman and Hobbies.

Page 32: Badge Brainteasers.
1) b. **2)** On the left arm. **3)** There are five Joining In badges. **4)** The Chief Scout's Silver Award. **5)** Promise Challenge, Community Challenge, Fitness Challenge, Creative Challenge, Global Challenge, Outdoor Challenge. **6)** The five Activity Badges are a: Scientist, b: Navigator, c: Entertainer, d: DIY, e: Air Activities. **7)** Look after a pet for at least three months: **e**, do a Sargent Jump: **f**, design and make a greetings card: **c**, show how to use the Green Cross Code: **d**, sew on a badge or button: **g**, know how to protect your home from fire: **a**, have a simple conversation in another language: **b**. **8)** Climber is not a Cub Scout Activity Badge.

Page 36: Quick Quiz.
1) Pacific Ocean (also the largest), Indian Ocean, Arctic Ocean, Southern Ocean. **2)** a: 70 per cent

Page 50: Bicycle Know-how

Saddle
Handlebars
Tyre
Pedal
Chain

D S N K S T T D D
L C A N U O E A P
F F A U M B Q E O
I E Y A S F I R T
B R T O N A J B A
N O C A B O G X T
D B V E S M I E O
E G G G Z L D N Y
E G N L Z F U J O

Page 59: The Big Quiz.
1. c. 2. b. 3. Six gold medals. 4. The answer is all of them! 5. b. 6. Astronaut Neil Armstrong. 7. b. 8. a. 9. a. 10. b.

Picture credits

All illustrations by David Parkins. All photographs © The Scout Association except as below.
Stuart Cox: 5b, 6b, 7t&b, 12, 13t, 14l, 37b, 39 (all), 44t&b, 45t&bl
Shutterstock.com: Viktor1: 13b, oksix: 14tr, Givaga: 14mr, mylisa:15t, brulove: 15b (banana), Kucher Serhii: 15b (apple), bajinda: 15b (strawberry), tehcheesiong: 15b (grapes), digieye: 16 (background), Taverina: 18b, wavebreakmedia: 19b, AISPIX by Image Source: 22, Tischenko Irina: 22 (background), jeka84: 24 (background), BMJ: 25tl, Eric Isselee: 25tr, Pan Xunbin: t5ml, basel101658: 25bl, Steve McWilliam: 25br, Tungphoto: 26 (paper), Scruggelgreen: 26 (coins), Gayvoronskaya_Yana: 34 (background), iofoto: 38t, serg_dibrova: 38 (bubbles), Suppakij1017: 40 (background), Korionov: 41b, Artur Aliev: 43 (background), Alan49: 46bl, Khomulo Anna: 46b, tkemot: 47m, Attl Tibor: 48tr, Susan Leggett: 48br, Hodag Media: 49br, Rob KEMP: 50tl, Bartlomiej Nowak: 50tm, Rafal Olkis: 50tr, Horiyan: 50b, pio3: Nils Jorgensen/Rex Features: 51, 51tl, Featureflash: 51bl&r, pirita: 53mr, Kletr: 54, Mark Bridger: 55t, Risto Viita: 55bl, irin-k: 55br, Pavel K: 56 (background), IrinaK: Back Page Images/Rex Feature: 58, 59tr, Warren Photographic Ltd: 25mr, US Coastal Service: 35t, Jane Mingay: 35b, Laura Kidd/Wikimedia Commons: 36t, theblaze. com: 36m, NASA: 40, 42t&m, Wikimedia Commons: 45br

What was the best thing you did this year?

Draw yourself doing your favourite activity.

....

....

....

....

....

....

What badges did you earn?

....

....

....

What are you looking forward to next year?

....

....

....

....